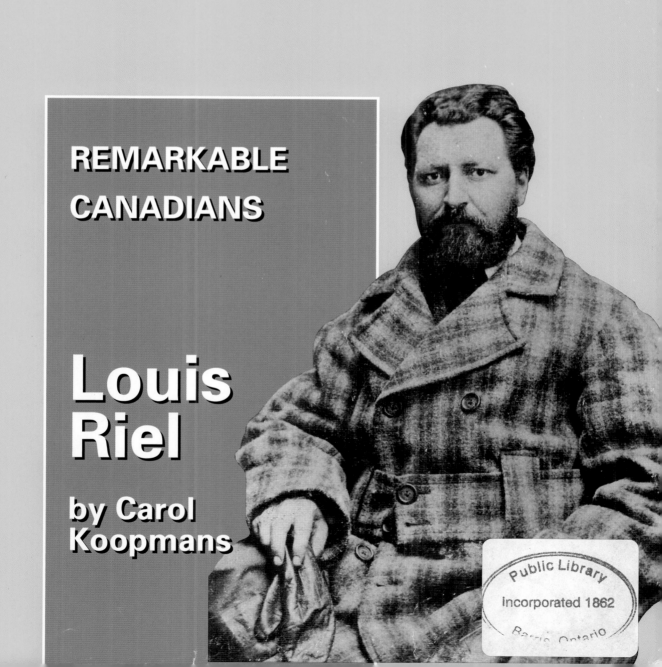

REMARKABLE CANADIANS

Louis Riel

by Carol Koopmans

Published by Weigl Educational Publishers Limited
6325 10 Street SE
Calgary, Alberta, Canada
T2H 2Z9

Website: www.weigl.com

All of the Internet URLs given in the book were valid at the time of publication.
However, due to the dynamic nature of the Internet, some addresses may have
changed, or sites may have ceased to exist since publication. While the author and
publisher regret any inconvenience this may cause readers, no responsibility for any
such changes can be accepted by either the author or the publisher.

Library and Archives Canada Cataloguing in Publication data available upon request.
Fax (403) 233-7769 for the attention of the Publishing Records department.

ISBN 978-1-55388-454-5 (hard cover)
ISBN 978-1-55388-455-2 (soft cover)

Printed in the United States of America
1 2 3 4 5 6 7 8 9 0 12 11 10 09 08

Editor: Heather C. Hudak
Design: Terry Paulhus

Photograph Credits
Alamy: pages 6, 19; Canadian Heritage Gallery/www.canadianheritage.com: page 18
(#21943/Archives of Ontario/S271); Getty Images: pages 3, 5 back, 7 top left, 7 top
middle, 7 top right, 7 bottom left, 8, 13 bottom, 14; Glenbow Archives: pages 1
(NA-789-52), 5 front (NA-2631-2), 12 (NA-1480-2), 20 (NA-47-28); Library and
Archives Canada: page 15 (a074103), 16 (C-015282), 17 (C-002424); The Manitoba
Museum: page 10; Provincial Archives of Alberta: page 9.

Every reasonable effort has been made to trace ownership and to obtain
permission to reprint copyright material. The publishers would be pleased
to have any errors or omissions brought to their attention so that they may
be corrected in subsequent printings.

We gratefully acknowledge the financial support of the Government of Canada
through the Book Publishing Industry Development Program (BPIDP) for our
publishing activities.

Contents

Who Is Louis Riel?

Louis Riel was the founding father of Manitoba. In the 1880s, he helped the **Métis** secure equal rights to own their land, to speak French, and to build Catholic schools. Riel worked tirelessly for this cause. He dreamed of building a nation that would guarantee the rights of all citizens living within its borders. All Canadians have benefited from this vision. Though he was hanged for **treason** in 1885, Canadians consider Riel a pioneer in the advancement of rights for all people, especially minorities.

> *"All that I have done and risked…rested certainly on the conviction that I was called upon to do something for my country…"*

Growing Up

Canada had not yet become a nation when Louis Riel was born on October 22, 1844. Riel had 11 brothers and sisters, but only nine lived to adulthood. As the oldest, Riel was a role model for his siblings.

Riel grew up among the French-Canadian and Métis in the parish of St. Boniface, near Lower Fort Garry. His parents were well-respected in the community. Riel's father was a strong supporter for the use of both the French and English languages in the courts.

Riel's parents were of French, British, and **Aboriginal** ancestry, and he grew up learning the customs of each of these cultures. He learned about French culture from his mother, Julie Lagimodière. Riel learned about Métis customs from his father. He learned to speak fluent French, Cree, and some English. Riel could move easily between cultures.

Today, Riel House is a National Historic Site of Canada.

Manitoba Tidbits

TREE
White Spruce

BIRD
Great Grey Owl

FLOWER
Crocus

The name "Manitoba" comes from the Cree words *Manitou bou*. This means "the narrows of the Great Spirit."

Until 1870, Manitoba was part of Rupert's Land. This land was owned by the Hudson's Bay Company (HBC) and included present-day Saskatchewan, and parts of Alberta, Ontario, Nunavut, and Quebec.

Fort Garry became the site for Manitoba's capital city, Winnipeg.

About 1.2 million people live in Manitoba.

Think about it!

Louis Riel grew up in the French-speaking Métis parish of St. Boniface in the Red River Settlement. By 1860, 10,000 Métis and 1,600 First Nations lived in the Red River Settlement. Think about the place where you live. Who were the first settlers? When did they arrive, and how did they live? Now, think about the place where you live today. How has it changed over time? What cultures live in your city or town? Make a chart comparing life today to life for the pioneers of your community.

Practice Makes Perfect

Riel was raised to have great respect for the Roman Catholic Church. His family worshipped at church regularly. When he began to attend school, the nuns and priests soon noticed Riel's gift for learning. They helped and encouraged him. Riel was quick-thinking, curious, and kind. His parents prayed that he would choose to become a priest.

When Riel was not studying, helping with chores, or playing, he liked to listen to the **elders** tell stories. Many talked of newcomers arriving in the area. These people came from the eastern parts of Canada and Great Britain to farm the land. The arrival of these **homesteaders** on Métis land caused concern. While the Métis had farmed and hunted in the area for many years, they had no proof of ownership or laws to protect their claims to the land. Riel witnessed these concerns first-hand.

When Riel was 14 years old, Bishop Taché, a priest at his school, sent him to attend Montreal College in Quebec. This was a rare opportunity, and the town had high expectations of Riel.

❧ The Red River Settlement was located along the Red and Assiniboine Rivers in what is now known as Manitoba and North Dakota.

Travel to the college was difficult. It took six weeks by oxcart, steamboat, and rail to reach Montreal. Slowly, Riel settled into life at Montreal College. He studied the Greek classics, Latin, philosophy, and religion. He was a serious student, forceful speaker, and gifted **orator**.

In 1864, Riel received word that his father had died. He had not seen his father while studying in Montreal, and the news devastated Riel. Three months before his graduation, Riel began to lose interest in his studies. He stopped living at the college and moved to a nearby **convent**. For a time, Riel continued to attend school. However, he missed a number of classes and was no longer welcome as a student at the college.

Before returning to Manitoba in 1868, Riel worked many jobs and spent some time living in the United States.

Key Events

In 1868, the Hudson's Bay Company planned to sell Rupert's Land to the newly formed government of Canada. Many Métis were upset by this decision. They did not have a title to the land and could not prove they owned it. The Métis worried that British homesteaders would take over their land, and force their language and culture on the Metis.

To voice their concerns, the Métis founded the Métis National Assembly. As secretary of the assembly, Riel warned the government that an attempt to gain control of the Red River Settlement would meet with resistance if the government did not first negotiate with the Métis. Still, the government tried to enter the area.

In November 1869, Riel and his supporters took over Fort Garry. They set up a **provisional** government and, over the next few months, negotiated their terms for joining **Confederation**, including the Métis List of Rights. The Red River Resistance of 1870 ended successfully with the creation of Manitoba. Following the resistance, Riel moved to the United States. He was **exiled** by the government in 1875. Nine years later, Riel returned to the area now known as Saskatchewan to lead the **North-West Resistance**.

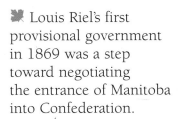 Louis Riel's first provisional government in 1869 was a step toward negotiating the entrance of Manitoba into Confederation.

Thoughts from Riel

Riel gave a number of speeches and wrote many letters. Here are some of the things he said.

Riel has a vision for the future.

"My people will sleep for one hundred years, but when they awake, it will be the artists who give them their spirit back."

Riel died for what he believed in.

"I have nothing but my heart and I have given it long ago to my country."

Riel wanted to pass Métis history on to future generations.

"We must cherish our inheritance. We must preserve our nationality for the youth of our future. The story should be written down to pass on."

Riel hoped the Red River Settlement would grow while he was in exile.

"Pray that God may preserve the little Métis nation, and cause it to grow."

Riel met with government representatives.

"As soon as we understood each other we joined in demanding what our English fellow subjects, in common with us, believe to be our just rights."

Riel felt strongly about Métis issues.

"No matter what happens now, the rights of the Métis are assured by the Manitoba Act: That is what I wanted—my mission is finished."

What Is a Leader?

Leaders are often people who have a strong vision and want to achieve specific goals. They use their education, experience, and skills to reach these goals. Leaders may be people who draw attention to important issues that impact people around the world.

Many Métis consider Louis Riel to be a hero. He was a leader who sought equal rights for the Métis and a leader who guided and inspired others. Louis Riel was a political leader. He was elected to represent the Métis as they challenged the government for their rights or freedoms.

❧ Despite being exiled, Riel was elected to the Manitoba legislature three times while he was in exile.

Leaders 101

Todd Ducharme

Achievements In 1986, Todd received a bachelor degree in law from the University of Toronto, and five years later he completed a master's degree in law from Yale Law School. After many years of university, Todd became a lawyer. In 2004, he became the first Métis appointed to the Ontario Superior Court of Justice as a Canadian judge.

Christi Belcourt (1966–)

Achievements Christi works as an artist, art teacher, and author. Her pictures celebrate the beauty in nature. Respectful of her Métis **heritage**, Christi studied the traditional use of plants and wrote *Medicines to Help Us.* Christi's work hangs in the permanent collections of the Thunder Bay Art Gallery and the Canadian Museum of Civilization. Christi's art has received awards from the Canada Council for the Arts, the Ontario Arts Council, and the Métis Nation of Ontario.

Douglas Cardinal (1934–)

Achievements Douglas Cardinal is a well-known architect. Strong, curvy lines are a feature of his buildings. In 1999, the Royal Architectural Institute of Canada awarded him a gold medal. This is the highest honour given to architects in Canada. By 2000, he had been awarded seven honourary doctorates in recognition of his contribution to architecture. He received the Governor General's Award for Visual and Media Arts in 2001.

Maria Campbell (1940–)

Achievements As a children's book writer, Maria tells stories about the traditional ways of the Métis. Some of her best-known books include *People of the Buffalo, Riel's People,* and *Little Badger and the Fire Spirit.* In 1979, Maria became Writer-in-Residence at the University of Alberta.

Métis List of Rights
The Métis wanted the Canadian government to consider their needs before they would agree to join Confederation. Under Riel's leadership, the provisional government drafted a List of Rights. Many of these rights were included in the Manitoba Act of 1870 when the province officially became part of Canada.

Influences

Of the many influences shaping Riel's life, the Catholic church played a major role. Those who knew or taught Riel said that Bishop Taché had the greatest impact. Taché had arrived from Montreal just after Riel was born. Over the years, Bishop Taché recognized Riel's potential for leadership. He became a **mentor** to Riel. Taché picked Riel to attend the Catholic College of Montreal and found a sponsor to pay the costs.

Bishop Taché gave Riel guidance and direction in his daily life. He taught by example. Riel learned the importance of obedience, order, and hard work. Riel respected Bishop Taché, who was educated and well-spoken. Riel tried to be like Bishop Taché. This helped him succeed in his studies.

🍁 St. Boniface Cathedral, where Louis Riel is buried, has been rebuilt many times since the early 1800s.

During the later years of political struggle, Bishop Taché remained a force in Riel's life. Riel depended on him for opinions and advice. The government considered Bishop Taché the voice of reason and selected him to become a key negotiator between the government in Ottawa and the Métis. Taché helped to have Métis rights included in the Manitoba Act (1870). In doing so, he helped oversee the joining of parts of western Canada into Confederation.

ALEXANDRE-ANTONIN TACHÉ

Alexandre-Antonin Taché dedicated his life to being a pioneer missionary. Trained in Montreal to become a priest, he made the journey west by canoe. He reached the Red River Settlement in 1845. He arrived just as the Métis began their struggle for land and language rights.

Throughout the 1870s and 1880s, Taché travelled to western Canada to build Catholic missions. He also urged French Canadians from Quebec to settle the West. Following the North-West Resistance in 1885, Taché continued to support Riel's push for Métis rights. He campaigned for separate Catholic schools and French language rights until his death in 1894.

Taché was an important figure in the development of the Roman Catholic Church in western Canada.

Overcoming Obstacles

In 1875, Riel was exiled for his leadership role in the Red River Resistance, and he fled to Montana in the United States. There, Riel became a spokesperson for the Montana Métis. He married and became a U.S. citizen. Riel planned to earn a living by teaching and farming.

During the time Riel lived in the United States, about 6,000 Métis left the Red River area to settle in Saskatchewan. Soon, homesteaders began moving to this area as well. Again, the Métis had no legal proof that the land was theirs. The Canadian government began to survey the land, and tensions increased. The Métis held mass meetings and sent petitions to the government. Their pleas were ignored.

About this same time, many homesteaders were also unhappy with the government. They thought the Canadian Pacific Railway (CPR) charged too much to ship grain east. They also felt that the government had given too much land to the Hudson's Bay Company and the CPR. Homesteaders wanted changes in the government.

Gabriel Dumont played a leading military role in the Saskatchewan Métis resistance during the North-West Resistance in 1885.

In 1884, Gabriel Dumont, a Métis leader, travelled to Montana to ask for Riel's help in gaining land claims for Saskatchewan Métis. Riel accepted Dumont's offer to return to Batoche, Saskatchewan.

Riel met with homesteaders, Métis, and First Nations about their concerns. Under Riel's leadership, they drew up a petition to send to the government. When they did not receive a response, Riel and his supporters set up a provisional government at Batoche. The homesteaders refused to take part. A week later, authorities were sent to arrest Riel.

In response, Gabriel organized an army, and violence broke out. Prime Minister John A. Macdonald sent 5,000 troops to the area. These Canadian forces defeated the Métis at Batoche. Riel surrendered. He was found guilty of treason for his role in the North-West Resistance and was hanged on November 16, 1885.

❦ The Battle of Batoche ended the North-West Resistance. After three days of fighting, the Métis and their supporters were defeated.

Achievements and Successes

One of Riel's most important achievements was his role in Manitoba joining Confederation. On July 15, 1870, Manitoba became the fifth province of Canada. The Manitoba Act outlined an acceptable agreement between the Métis and the Canadian government. It granted a Bill of Rights recognizing the status of both French and English as official languages. The bill included the right for Catholics and Protestants to set up their own school systems. Riel feared that Métis would become the forgotten people of Canada. The Manitoba Act of 1870 secured their identity by recognizing their language and religion.

To end Métis resistance, Sir John A. Macdonald agreed to nearly all of the terms outlined in the Métis "List of Rights" of 1869.

The North-West Resistance at Batoche in 1885 became the last military battle on Canadian soil. Riel surrendered at Batoche, and the struggle for minority rights moved from the battlefield into the courtroom. This meant that future generations could challenge their rights through the legal system.

In 1992, Riel's contributions to Confederation were recognized. The House of Commons officially named Riel the Founding Father of Manitoba. Stories, songs, poems, books, and plays salute his deeds. Schools, buildings, parks, and streets bear his name. A statue of Riel stands on the Manitoba legislative ground.

LOUIS RIEL DAY

The Manitoba government declared that Louis Riel Day will be celebrated on the third Monday in February each year. This day honours the Founding Father of Manitoba and his legacy. Manitoba legislated this holiday to **commemorate** the anniversary of Louis Riel's death. It provides an official day to recognize Riel's struggles and his contributions in building the province. "The Journey Home" was the theme for the first holiday celebration held in 2008. Following the Battle at Batoche, Riel gave his sash to a family that had let him hide in their basement. Shortly after, Riel surrendered to General Middleton, military commander of the Canadian troops. The sash was "brought home" to Manitoba as part of the first Louis Riel Day events. To find out more about the Louis Riel holiday, visit **http://web2.gov.mb.ca/laws/statutes/ 2007/c01807e.php**.

Write a Biography

A person's life story can be the subject of a book. This kind of book is called a biography. Biographies describe the lives of remarkable people, such as those who have achieved great success or have done important things to help others. These people may be alive today, or they may have lived many years ago. Reading a biography can help you learn more about a remarkable person.

At school, you might be asked to write a biography. First, decide who you want to write about. You can choose a leader, such as Louis Riel, or any other person you find interesting. Then, find out if your library has any books about this Learn as much as you can about her. Write down the key events person's life. What was this person's childhood like? What he or she accomplished? What are his or her goals? What makes this person special or unusual?

A concept web is a useful research tool. Read the questions in the following concept web. Answer the questions in your notebook. Your answers will help you write your biography

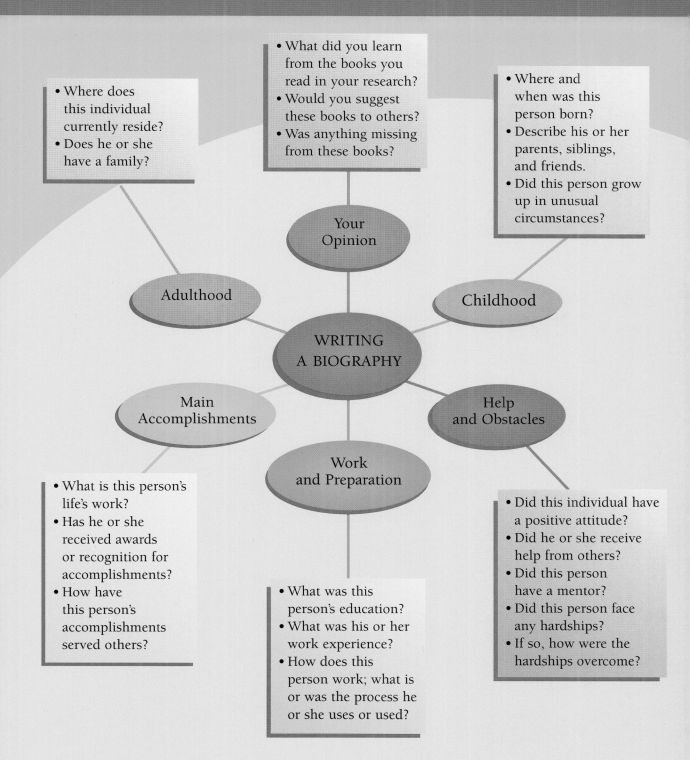

- Where does this individual currently reside?
- Does he or she have a family?

- What did you learn from the books you read in your research?
- Would you suggest these books to others?
- Was anything missing from these books?

- Where and when was this person born?
- Describe his or her parents, siblings, and friends.
- Did this person grow up in unusual circumstances?

Your Opinion

Adulthood

Childhood

WRITING A BIOGRAPHY

Main Accomplishments

Help and Obstacles

Work and Preparation

- What is this person's life's work?
- Has he or she received awards or recognition for accomplishments?
- How have this person's accomplishments served others?

- What was this person's education?
- What was his or her work experience?
- How does this person work; what is or was the process he or she uses or used?

- Did this individual have a positive attitude?
- Did he or she receive help from others?
- Did this person have a mentor?
- Did this person face any hardships?
- If so, how were the hardships overcome?

Timeline

YEAR	LOUIS RIEL	WORLD EVENTS
1844	Riel is born in 1844 in St. Boniface, Manitoba.	European homesteaders arrive at the Red River Settlement.
1858	Riel attends Montreal College to study and prepare for the priesthood.	India comes under the control of Great Britain.
1865	Riel takes job as a law clerk in Montreal.	U.S. President Abraham Lincoln is assassinated.
1869	Riel is elected secretary of the Métis National Assembly in the Red River Settlement.	The Transcontinental Railway in the United States is completed.
1870	Riel is elected President of the Provisional Government for Rupert's Land and the Northwest Territories.	Sir John A. Macdonald accepts the Métis List of Rights, and Manitoba becomes the fifth province in Confederation.
1880	Riel becomes the spokesperson for the Montana Métis.	Bison are nearly extinct.
1885	The Métis lose the Battle of Batoche, and Riel is hanged for treason.	The Canadian Pacific Railway nears completion.

Further Research

How can I find out more about Louis Riel?

Most libraries have computers that connect to a database that contains information on books and articles about different subjects. You can input a key word and find material on the person, place, or thing you want to learn more about. The computer will provide you with a list of books in the library that contain information on the subject you searched for. Non-fiction books are arranged numerically, using their call number. Fiction books are organized alphabetically by the author's last name.

Websites

To learn more about Louis Riel, visit
http://metisresourcecentre.mb.ca

For a slide show about
Louis Riel's life, check out
www.metismuseum.ca/
riel_05750/Louis_Riel2.html

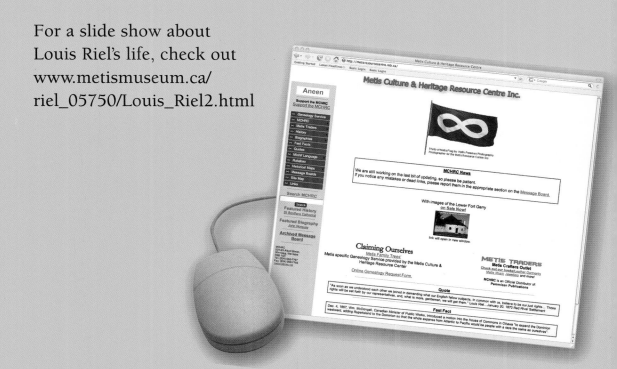

Words to Know

Aboriginal: original inhabitants of a country

commemorate: to honour the memory of a person or event

Confederation: the creation of Canada in 1867

convent: a community made up of people who are devoted to their religious views

elders: the older and more influential members of a community

exiled: barred from one's home or country

heritage: the people, places, and culture of the past

homesteaders: people who built homes and buildings on plots of land

mentor: a wise and trusted teacher

Métis: children of European and Aboriginal unions

North-West Resistance: an uprising of Métis and First Nations peoples in Saskatchewan in 1885

orator: a person who is skilled at public speaking

provisional: temporary

resistance: an attempt to prevent something

treason: the act of betraying one's country

Index